EVERYTHING IS FUCKED FOREVER

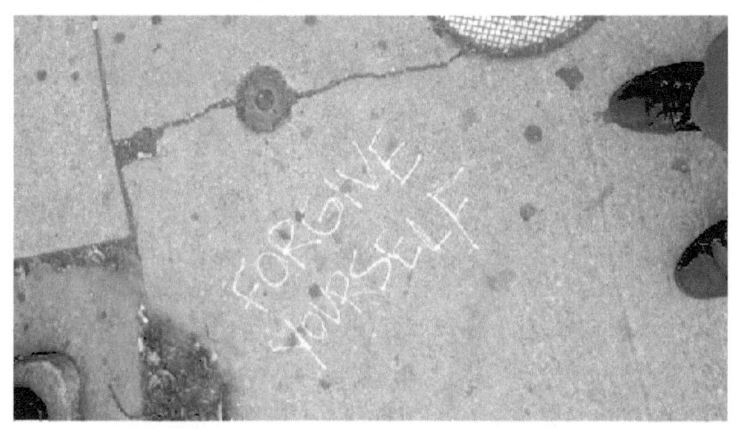

Jay Miller

In loving memory of Andrew Michael Letcher and Harris Lee Wittels. Within six months we lost them both to the same demon, I will never forget how much both of you made me laugh.

Huge thanks to my brother Roy Miller, without his help I could have never put this together. He is the hot sauce on my burrito.

I would also like to thank my best friend Danielle Jordan who constantly motivates me to be a better person and achieve more.

■ ■ ■

"I never cared so much about making perfect sense. I wanted to make perfect nonsense. I wanted to tell jokes, but I didn't give a fuck about the punch line."

- Harmony Korine

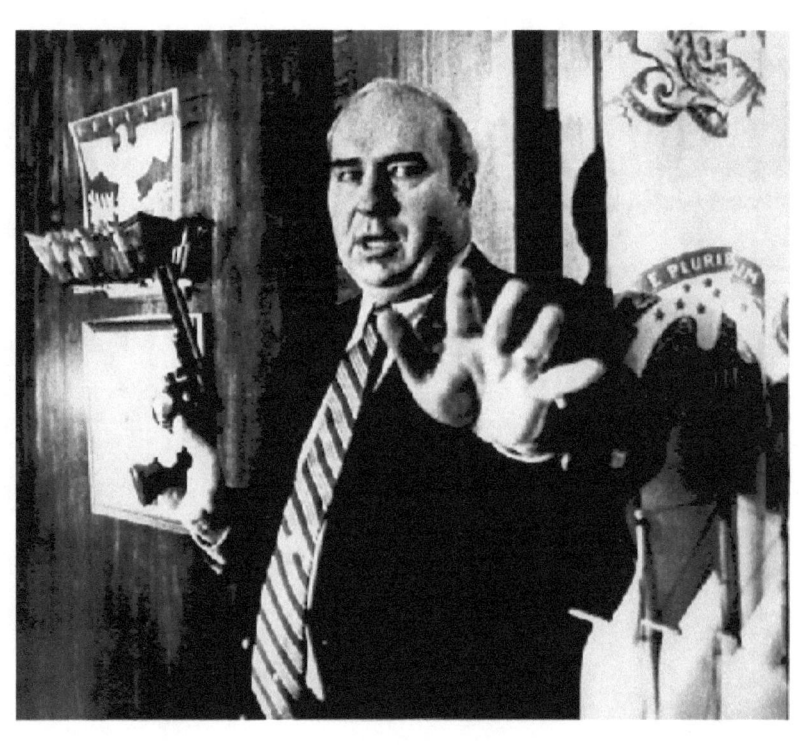

"PLEASE, PLEASE LEAVE THE ROOM IF THIS WILL...IF THIS WILL AFFECT YOU."

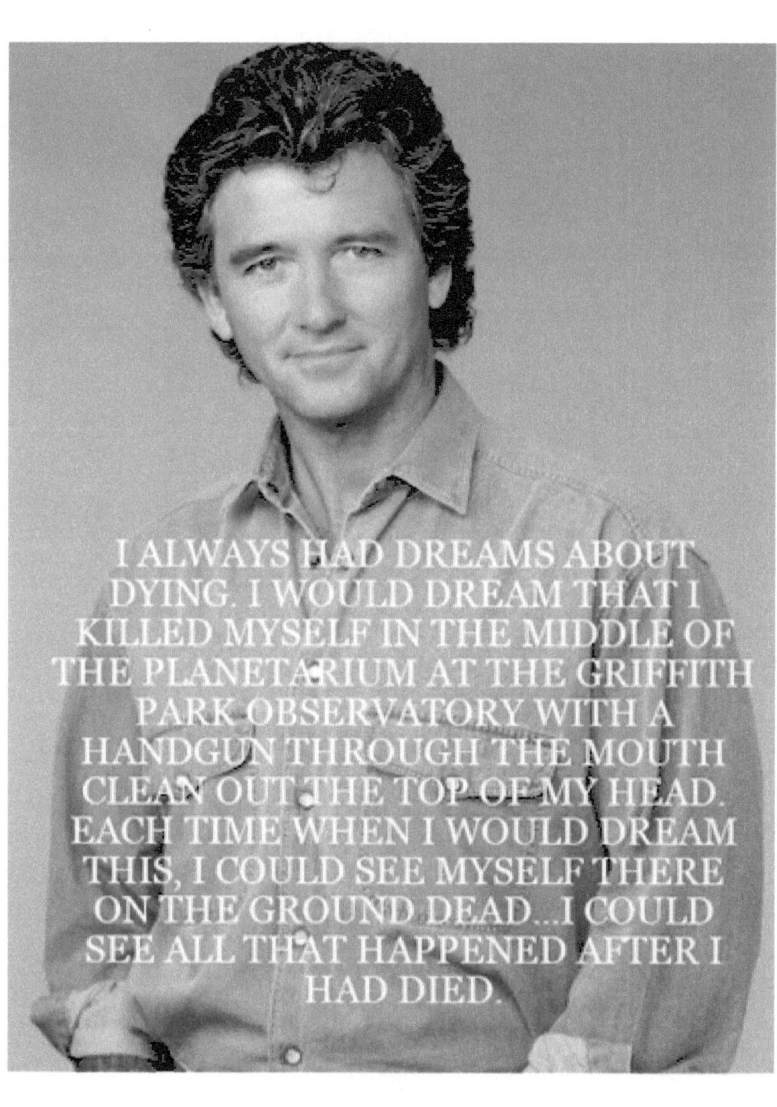

Drugstore

I was molested today by a woman who was probably close to 70 years of age. I was at the drugstore to purchase sleeping pills and beer because I live at home with my mom and she snores so fucking loud even the neighbors have to drug themselves to get to sleep at night. I had already selected my beer and I was carefully reading the ingredients of all the different sleep aids this place had to offer. It was a full spectrum rainbow of coma inducing drugs. Liquids, liquid capsules, solid capsules, chewable capsules, chewable gummies, even dissolving strips that you put on your tongue.

I was reading the back of one of the containers of solid capsules when this old bag stepped up beside me quite close. I didn't pay much attention at first, I pretty much always assume that most old people are fucking looney or just plain lonely and starved for attention. As she scooted a bit closer that annoying song "Without you" by Harry Nilsson was playing over the store's sound system and I could feel the awkwardness building between the old hag and myself. This song was originally Performed by Badfinger and was the main cause of their guitarist/vocalists death in 1983. A quarrel over the ASCAP royalties for the song took place over the phone with one of his band mates and he hung himself in his

As I decide on a sleeping drug this old bag reaches over and brushes my bum with her right hand, I pretend to not notice at first but then she does it again, firm grab this time. A right proper squeeze to my ass cheek. There isn't any way I can even try to pretend that it hadn't just happened. Now we are staring at each other face to face. Me and this horny old coot. I am thinking to myself, what the hell? I could probably just do her proper right now in the handicapped bathroom and no one would even notice. We are still just kind of staring at each other.

Me with my beer and sleeping pills in my hands.

Her with her right hand planted on my ass.

This is especially strange because two nights earlier I had somewhat of a lucid dream about fucking an old lady in the handicapped bathroom of a drugstore that started out pretty much exactly like what is happening here. The old bitch in my dream was a tad more attractive but I kept thinking, what the hell, I could always just close my eyes and pound it home.

I can't live, if living is without you. I can't give, I can't give anymore...

The song is still playing on and these thoughts are still racing through my head as we stand there still, her hand on my ass and me feeling very confused. Confused and slightly turned on. A few more moments pass and I shift my ass from her grip, smile politely and walk away from her saying "Have a nice day, mam".

I walk to the counter, pay for my beer and sleeping drugs and exit the store, the whole while still thinking of how I probably could have just nailed that grandma in a public bathroom and wondering to myself if it would have been any good.

Radioshack

I always have trouble waking up in the morning no matter how long I have been sleeping for but I find once I am up for the day, I am usually always glad that I experienced morning. Lately I have been having a vivid dream. Over and over, I wake up and I am about to face a first day at a brand new job that I am totally not at all excited about...at, Lets say...Radioshack. So, I keep constantly waking with the fear of "fuck, I don't want to fucking work at Radioshack!", you know?

Its like when were young and in school how that first morning at the end of summer felt, except now you work at Radioshack. Being an adult is like a running gag joke that no one fucking gets and it is always pissing everyone off.

Then you die.

I always wanted to live next to a taffy factory. I have never really been sure if such a place exists, a factory where solely taffy is made. I have always made this well known to people, those I view as potential life mates or good friends. I always talk about shitty old taffy factories because I can close my eyes and envision walking down a road at dusk with my headphones on smelling taffy ever so lightly in the air. That's pretty fucked, right?

I would literally have intense imaginary moments in which the smell of fresh taffy in the air was the most amazing thing I had ever experienced. Like the feeling of super hot water on the top of your head dripping down your body on early mornings. That tingling sensation.

There were other times where I would have out of body experiences viewing my own life from the display of an MRI machine, just seeing the visual reaction to things as they happen. This was the kind of shit I didn't readily tell people.

I think that's also why my view of death is so out of whack. I like to sit around and think about all the possible things that can happen to our consciousnesses after we die. I honestly find death as a subject much more interesting than life.

Don't get me wrong. Life is amazing and I am glad to be experiencing it in all its shameful glory.Sometimes I do seriously have to ask myself if living is genuinely more interesting than all of the possibilities the death of the body holds. It's a hard one.

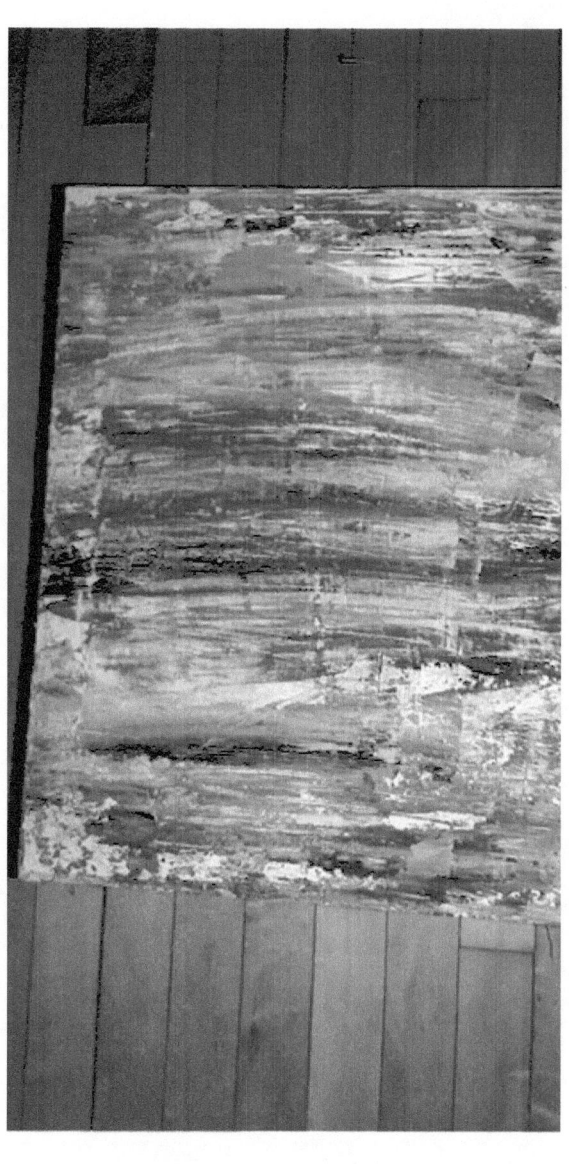

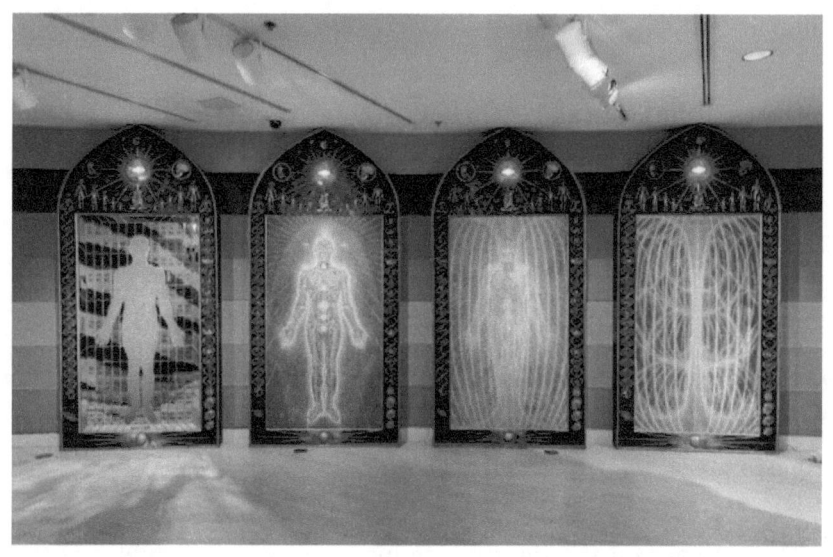

THE STRANGER ON THE LEFT
AND THE
STRANGER AND THE RIGHT

"You will know the entirety of the universe for the briefest of moments"

I think we were sitting on a ledge, or maybe the edge of a small cliff surrounded by a blinding nothingness. Two total strangers talking about the sensation they were sharing in that space and time. A random meeting of the conscience. Neither being sure of where they are or if their surroundings are even real, if the conversation is even happening.

"I am going to tell you something" a mysterious invisible presence announces.

"You will die again and again but never be reborn"

The stranger on the right turns his head toward the stranger on the left as the stranger on the left continues to stare forward.

The stranger on the right desires eye contact.

It is remembering how to relate, or it is learning how to for the first time in this new form and place.

The stranger on the right places his hand on the shoulder of the stranger on the left. The stranger on the left slowly turns his head towards the stranger on the right. Their eyes meet for the first time.

They have been speaking for what seems like an eternity, both staring forward off the edge of this cliff or ledge or whatever it was on the edge of what was everything and nothing all at once and this was the first time they had seen each other.

The stranger on the left and the stranger on the right are identical.

This fact is lost on them however because they are unaware of their own outward appearance completely. Both of the strangers hold eye contact, their lips quiver and they cry for a brief second. Slowly, they both turn their heads back to their original forward facing direction. What seems like a washed out sunrise occurs and everything has suddenly became much brighter.

"When you wake up you will never be capable of want again. The need for trivial things will become obsolete. Time will move at a different pace and you will never be the same again" said the same mysterious voice from before.

Both strangers started to explore their visual surroundings more and more. Looking from side to side, up and down. The vast nothingness had turned back into a real physical place but everything was out of proportion, fuzzy and grainy.

The two strangers once again began staring into their eyes, this time realizing that they were one in the same. The most amazing feeling of warmth entered their shared consciousness and the entire universe became still. Everything slowly started to come back into focus.
"YOU NEED TO COME BACK NOW"

The stranger on the right felt himself fall away and then crawling out through the mouth of the stranger on the left, stepping out through his throat into the real world, closing his eyes for just a moment and releasing a single tear.

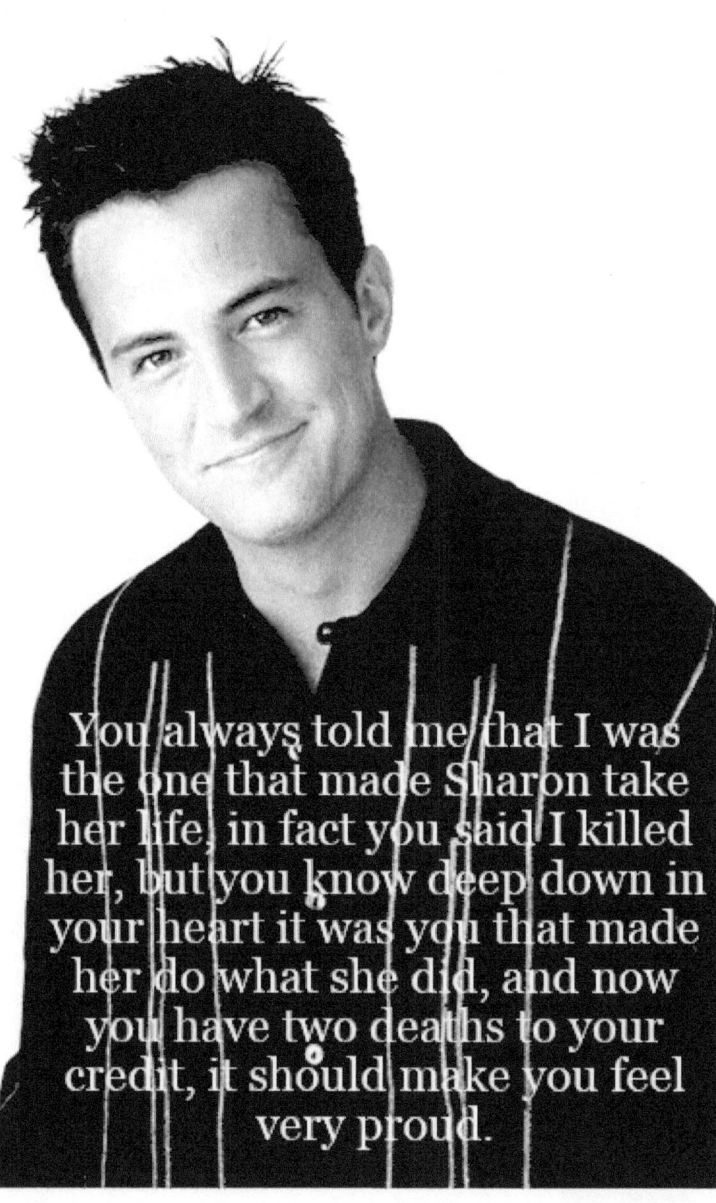

You always told me that I was the one that made Sharon take her life, in fact you said I killed her, but you know deep down in your heart it was you that made her do what she did, and now you have two deaths to your credit, it should make you feel very proud.

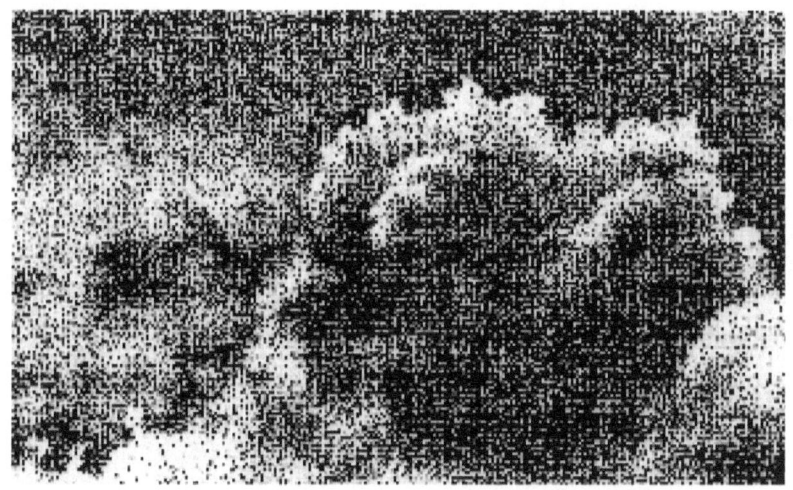

SO YOUR BIG BLACK CLOUD WILL COME....

When we are born we see the world upside down. It's scientifically proven. We really do see the world upside down, it is our brain.... constantly working to reverse the image of what our eyes see to deliver the world to us right side up.

PART ONE - "SOME KIND OF FOREIGN JOB"

Looking back at it now it's like seeing the same movie over and over again but with little differences each time. It's hard to even realize what elements have changed each time I flash back to my life because they hit so slightly at first...it's like this alternate reality where everything in life was how I would have liked it to be and then after i re-live it enough, everything has completely changed back to how it really happened. It was like what deja vu used to feel like when I was alive.

It's September 10th 1993, I'm standing on the corner of Chicago and Damen. The sun is shining really bright and it seems like it's around

80 degrees or so. I immediately remember this moment from my life, although in reality it was raining very hard and especially cold for September. People are passing by rapidly...not a lot of people (wasn't really a busy time of day) but they are all moving very fast. I don't seem to be heading in any particular direction. Just pacing slowly in circles, waiting by the diner on the corner. Smoking a cigarette and pacing. This is the diner that give me food poisoning so bad I was puking blood. Lorraine's Diner "We have dirty dishes and bitchy waitresses but damn good food" that was their motto when I was alive.

A car slows down and pulls up by the sidewalk in front of the diner.

"SHIT"

I'm splashed with water out of nowhere and all of the sudden it's pouring rain in a split second. I look around and it seems to have been raining all afternoon, everything is drenched, puddles are swallowing the concrete whole, all the way up to the curb. I step up to the passenger door and wait for it to be unlocked.

I'm starting to slowly realize these small differences between the way my brain wants me to perceive my past and the way things actually happened. I'm seamlessly integrating reality back into my afterlife. It's pouring rain all around me and I was splashed by a puddle as my father's car ever so gracefully pulled up the curbside... but I am completely dry.

My dad seems flustered.

I know why we are here, sitting in this parked car by the side of the road. Rain pouring onto the windshield in silver dollar sized blots that increase at least twice their size as they splash down in front of us. We are here to force words that won't mean anything. To continue a charade we had been acting out for over a decade.

My mother just died.

So, we are going to go through these motions like pre-programmed artificial beings. We will go over a few fond memories. Smile a bit, probably cry a little.

He will say "I love you".

I will say "I love you too, dad" and it won't be until I step out of the car back onto the street corner that I will realize, deep down, I really do mean it.

All of this happening in a parked car in the rain two blocks from my apartment. Six blocks from my dad's house. Four blocks from where my mother had been living. My dad will shake my hand. Even though at this point I have no concept of time I am fully aware that this is the first time I have seen this man in a long while.

I will never see him again.

He lived just eight blocks away from me.

I know this is exactly what happened because I lived it. I lived it and then re- "lived" it. Over and over and over and over. I don't know how long I have been replaying these memories in my mind. I don't know because there is no sense of time. I just float back and forth between memories from my life and each time they become a bit more real, a bit more how they actually happened...just a bit more somber each time.

The first memory I went back to was that day in the car with my dad. The first time I went back to it, it played out much differently from start to finish. It was like the neighborhood was glowing. Buildings were so clean they shimmered.

You know how sometimes you wake up feeling great and you don't know why? You just wake up and leave your house to go face to the day and for some reason this one day it's so much easier than every other day. The sun may be shining especially bright or maybe you caught the bus within just a few minutes of standing at each stop. It is just one of those days where you seem to be coming up all around. That's how it was the first time I came back to this day with my pops.

People around me were walking casually, smiling and holding hands just enjoying the beauty of the day. I have no idea how I even knew I was there, in that moment where he told my my mother was dead but somehow I did. Haven't you ever had someone tell you something that should have shocked or surprised you and it just...didn't?

A really nice car pulls up to the curb and I don't even get splashed by shitty, scummy rain/sewer water.

In reality my dad drove an 89 Ford Tempo.

This was definitely not my dad's tempo. This was some kind of foreign job, a real piece of european automotive technology. Something my dad, or anyone in my family for that matter, could not afford.

He reaches over and opens the door for me from the inside with a forced smile that almost looks painful. He looks really healthy. No age lines and gross teeth from cigarettes.

He puts the car in drive and we pull away.

On the drive to wherever we were going, he breaks the news to me.

Dad hits a button on the dash of his foreign job and a garage door opens underneath a nice triple high flat near the north shore. Not many words have been spoken since he told me of my mother's passing. We exit the car and head up to where he is living in my death dream.

He lives on the second floor and it's surprisingly even bigger than it seems. I can tell before I even enter that it's going to be a ridiculously nice place. The kind of place I used to deliver food to downtown when I briefly worked for a taco joint on the southside in the summer of 1989.

I get a good look around and notice photos of my mother all over the apartment. I see her sewing machine in the corner of the room. There are nice things everywhere. Big screen TV, laser disc player. It is apparent to me that my mother was still living here when she died yesterday morning. My parents were still together.

My dad grabs a beer for each of us and we sit down on a leather sectional. Probably the nicest couch I had ever seen. A couch much nicer than anything my real father could have ever afforded. He worked his whole life and he worked hard. He worked hard for his own pride. He didn't care about recognition or promotions, he just took pride in what he did. As far as work ethic went, he was truly someone that myself and everyone else could have aspired to be.

As we drink our beers and sit in silence everything begins to blend into pure light. Slowly my dad is disappearing and I am left in an empty clouded void. An almost black void of near nothingness.

Each time my mind goes to this memory, my dad would look a bit more tired and ill. The nice things in the apartment would vanish, one by one until the apartment itself was no longer a part of the memory.

After a while we were just sitting silent in the car again. After a while, my memories shifted from back to what actually happened to that familiar black cloud.

PART TWO - "ONE LAST SHOT AT AN ARTIFICIAL HAPPINESS?"

When we die, our brain keeps working. Some may say its working harder than ever. Our heart has stopped beating, its stopped pumping blood through our body and our lungs have stopped taking in oxygen and breathing back out.

Supposedly our brain keeps jolting away for seven minutes.

How long is seven minutes when time has no meaning?

Im standing outside with some friends. it's the summer of 1991. I am 23 years old. I know this because my hair is down to my shoulders and i'm standing outside of crobar near chicagos state of the art housing project, Cabrini Green. Crobar was a rock bar at this point and we are here with the purpose of seeing a new local band, The Smashing Pumpkins.

My mouth is dry and I reek of pot. That's another way to be sure of the time and place I am currently occupying. I can actually taste the stale cigarettes on my lips. I have been here before in my memories. Mouth Breathing hipsters are surrounding me and breathing all of my air as we enter the club. I approach the bar and order a whiskey and coke. The only thing I will pay to drink at a bar.

A good friend of mine from my life buys a round of shots for all of us at the bar and proceeds to congratulate me on my engagement.

I was going to get married.

At 23 years old.

The first band that played was called seam. I had never heard them but really enjoyed their set and became more and more enthused towards everything as I continued to down whiskey and cokes. About halfway through their set a woman comes up from behind me and puts her arms around my body, kissing me on the neck. I turn around to a familiar face.

I smile at her smile and our faces proceed to attempt to bind themselves to each other forever with a sickeningly wet, drunken kiss which was immediately followed by some mockery from my shot downing friend. My fiance nor myself notice the heckling as we are so focused on the eyes and lips of each other.

This was the kind of love that a human only feels once during its existence. No matter where you are in your life and no matter how happy, settled or comfortable any one of you may be... You can surely remember that one love that got away that felt like no other love ever has or will. It is so rare for someone to actually spend the rest of their lives with the lover they truly should have and that small number of people are fortunate beyond words.

As the pumpkins took the stage we abandoned our drinks and bolted towards the front of the club. It was a small but excited crowd. The band had just released their first album and for all of us local music fans and aspiring musicians the record stood for something exciting. Perhaps the first time my group of friends had been seriously excited by music since first hearing Joy Divisions "Love will tear us apart" when we were all still wet behind the ears.

We danced and screamed and had fun all night. I held my fiance, my arms around her swaying to daydream, letting each note enter my body through my ear and travel all the way to my heart.

Each lyric sinking in and expressing what we weren't able to:

My daydream feels like one inside of you....

I could literally feel the rumbling of the speakers in the innermost part of my heart, those notes and words seemed to stretch out from my heart and wrap themselves through my arms into the heart of my woman. My lover. The better part of what I couldn't even ever hope to be.

I was excited....About music, about life and especially about falling in love and building a life as an adult with the woman I loved.

We were riding high. It felt like we were truly unstoppable and that life was just starting in that summer of 1991. We were stoned, drunk and flying on disco biscuits. The show ended with an explosion of epic rock. It was literally the best concert I had ever seen throughout my entire life but I would remember it forever, the tiny hazy bits that I could, for completely different reasons. In this vision though I remember it as a wonderful night with a wonderful girl that I loved and life was just fine.

We pulled out of our parking spot onto the street with a blast of speed, music blaring and our friends cheering us off into the night. We got home and feel asleep in eachothers arms, eagerly anticipating another day of life together. As I fell into rest I remember pressing the front of my face into the back of my fiance's head. An attempt to embrace her thoughts and try to share in her dreams the same way I happily shared in her life.

This was the first time I went back to this memory. Each time it has gotten darker and uglier.

I am at the club again. Constantly sniffling. Checking my nose for apparent evidence of my dirty deeds. I am antsy and I am buzzing and for me that is not a good combination. We are getting some shit from the door guy because my ID is expired. I am pissed as all hell because we are missing the first act. After about 15 minutes of complete horse shit we are allowed to enter the club. I am flashing inside my own mind as I walk inside. Buzzing on anger from the door guy's shit fit and beyond gone on dope and booze, I am already intent on a not so peaceful night. If I could talk to myself as a sober person at this moment, I would have plenty to say, although I know I wouldn't listen.

I had already snorted a copious amount of cocaine and inhaled a bottle of grain alcohol before coming to the show. I head straight to the bar and order a whiskey and coke and a shot of tequila. We are here to supposedly celebrate my engagement to my girlfriend. A situation I am not very enthusiastic about. I love her so deeply but she is pregnant and I am not so honestly employed. I desperately want to be a "husband" and a "father" I am really just not sure that I know how. My whole life this has been a problem for me, striving to be a better person than I am actually able or aware of how to be.

My fiance wanted to come to this show tonight but I insisted that it was a guys night out to "celebrate" my engagement to her. I just needed some time away. I just needed to get severely fucked up and let loose for a bit and the last thing I wanted to do was have her see me upset in any way. I was dead set on making this work, I may have been overwhelmed but I knew I just needed to get it out of my system.

She showed up anyway.

This set me off. I mean, I did love this girl but I was in the middle of an all out freakout. So I started taking things up a notch. I drank. I mean, I really drank. I was honestly excited to be there for this show and I didn't even turn around to look at the stage once while Corgan and company delivered their goods.

I was blackout drunk.

The pumpkins finish their set and the crowd begans to disperse. I hunch forward in my bar stool in the classic drunken fashion of forgetting how to actually stand up. I decide instead to just turn around and watch as all the people file out the front door past the bar. The room is spinning and I can't seem to find solid ground.

I am fucking drunk. Tweaking. Gone.

I grab my fiance by the wrist and storm out the club. She is obviously worried but she was a very peaceful and quiet woman. Thats one of the first things that attracted me to her. I tell her I love her very much and we need to go home. She says something to me about how she doesn't want to get in the car with me, something I probably should have listened more closely to since I loved her so much.

I start the car, put it in drive and peel out of my parking spot. I hit 80 miles an hour before I even really realized I had already pulled out of the parking lot. I peeled around the curve by Cabrini, twisting the wheel without breaking at all. The car slams into the traffic light by Halsted and wraps around it with a swift...

CRUNCH!

She was wrong, I didn't kill both of us.

But I did take two lives.

I walked away without a scratch and somehow only did 2 years in jail before I was let out under supervision. The judge said the maximum sentence could have been 30 years. It should have been life. They should have killed me.

PART THREE - "MANS BEST FRIEND"

The memories of my early childhood are even hazy in these visions. They come and go in a choppy manner that reminds me of the obscure indie films I enjoyed in my early twenties. The memories of days when my parents were together almost won't come. There is a sort of block on this period even in my subconscious.

However one particular event won't leave me no matter how hard I try to let it slip away. This memory has never been altered in my death dreams. It has played back the same exact way every Goddamn time. This is my earliest memory and I have a feeling it will eventually be the finale of my seven minutes before total death.

I was crushed.

It's hard to believe that we can grow so attached to animals. I had a dog named Mikey. He was my best friend. When I turned 5 years old my grandmother (just about 6 months before she died) took me out to lunch to celebrate. She took me to my favorite place to eat in the whole city. I got pancakes. I always got pancakes when I was with my grandma because she let me eat whatever I want. Our family didn't have much money and grandpa had left a nice chunk for grams before he kicked the bucket. She loved to spoil me when she could and I didn't mind.

Watching the butter melt onto the pancakes as grams pours my syrup on for me, as she always did. I can smell the maple and the sugar and the coffee in the air.

We sat and ate and talked for hours. We talked about my grandfather and his battle with cancer. She wanted me to know about him and pass his memory on with our family over the years. I think this was especially important due to her recent diagnosis (although as a child I didn't understand). We talked about my uncle and how my grandmother wanted me to know that he was also a great man (even though he was a vagrant and had been found dead of a drug overdose under a bridge in Baltimore the previous summer, another situation which at that age, I did not understand).

As we were leaving my grandmother asked me why I was always so quiet and seemed so sad. I opened up to her about the hard time I was having making friends and that I felt like no one liked me. Even though this was sad news to her, her face lit up. She knew right away what to do.

We got in the car and drove over to the pet store on Montrose. When she pulled up in front, I smiled. My grandma always understood me better than anyone else.

She said I could have any animal in the store no matter what my parents had to say, she would deal with them.

That's when I found Mikey.

Well, he wasn't named Mikey yet but he would be. He was an extremely ugly little fucker. A total mutt. He was small, stocky and really was ugly as sin. I knew right then this was my dog. My grandma took care of the business aspect of things as I got to know Mikey a little better. His nose was so wet and he slobbered everywhere while attempting to lick my face.

6 years later and I am 11 years old. I had made a few friends over the years but Mikey was still my closest confidant. He slept at my feet every night. It was my first experience with true love.

It was late on a summer night. The sun was still slightly out but it was well past 8PM. It was a thursday...I knew this because my dad gets out of work at 5 but never made it home before 8 on thursdays due to his mandatory stop off at the bar on the way home. Sitting down for a "beer or two" which actually meant getting shit faced until he could barely stand up off his stool to walk out to his piece of shit car and drive his sorry ass home.

Tensions had been high at our house for the last few weeks since my mother was laid off from her job as a school teacher. My dad had started drinking a lot more then usual and my mom was already starting to think about leaving him. He had never hit her. He really wasn't a violent man for most of my youth but sometimes people change. They don't want to but they do....

On this night my dad got home around 9 o'clock. I was sitting on the floor with Mikey watching some kind of terrible TV show trying to stay awake for him to get home. When my dad walked in Mikey jumped over and ran to greet him. Dancing happily at my father's feet, my best friend Mikey. I jump up also excited to greet my dad.

I could smell the booze from across the room and could sense my dad becoming angry at Mikey for barking although it was simply a playful, friendly greeting. Dad stumbled around a bit yelling at Mikey to "shut the fuck up" or he was going to "fucking kill him". These kinds of words were thrown around alot. It was kind of like a family tradition to get drunk and say things you didn't mean, a tradition I would carry on until the final day of my life.

My mom was locked back in her bedroom (dad had been sleeping on the couch for a couple weeks). Dad walked sloppily into the kitchen and began to eat a raw hotdog while mumbling to himself. I took Mikey in my arms and he could sense my worry. He jumped out of my arms and leaped towards my dad. Jumping around panting in circles at my dad's feet once again, all he wanted was a quick pat on the back or a playful petting.

It was then that my dad, the man who created me, picked up my tiny dog, my best fucking friend by the neck and slammed his tiny little head against the wall.

"I told that fucking dog to shut up"

This was the first and only time that words became actions and it would change the way I related to my father for the rest of my life.

My pops plopped down on the couch.

"Get me a beer" he said.

I stood there my back against the wall, not able to move. My best friend lying lifeless....his tiny body on the floor, his head resting partly on the wall it was smashed against. I got my dad a beer, picked up Mikey and knocked on my mom's door.

My dad had killed my best friend and it was then that my mother and I realized that if we didn't leave right then and there he probably would have killed us too. Sometimes people change. They don't want to but they do.

PART FOUR - "NINETEEN NINETY EIGHT"

In 1998 I was 30 years old. I had finally found a job I loved working at a record store on the city's northwest side. Since getting out of jail in 94 I had really began to look at my life. I had vowed to never be in another relationship again because I felt I did not deserve to be loved and also felt I had completely lost the ability to love another person. When you face something like being responsible for the loss of another's life, especially the one person who meant more to you then anyone in the world, life becomes a bit numb...all of the time.

My dad died in 1995 and I never got a chance to see him after the day he came to tell me about my mother's death. Actually, I had plenty of chances and so did he but neither one of us did anything about it. I still resented him for killing Mikey and he knew it.

This year, 1998 would be the last year of my life. I am not sure how I died but I know it happened fast because I was alive and feeling things and living new experiences until I seamlessly slipped into reliving my past as a fantasy.

It was quite amazing at first. All of the terrible things that had happened to me were being reimagined by my mind as much happier and exciting times. It was like having a second chance at life except I couldn't live a normal life, nothing happened in an order that made any sense. It was so random and flippant.

One minute I was a 6 year old and the next minute I was romanticizing losing my virginity as a much more exciting and passionate experience than it really was. Then back and forth and back and forth. The more and more I saw these events, the more they came to resemble the actual sad, pathetic story of my existence.

1998 was the last year my physical body would see.

PART FIVE - SEEING MY PEACE

All of my visions and memories up to this point had been based on real life experiences. This memory however had no place, no real origin other than in my imagination. It was everything I wanted out of life. It was my final happiness.

Somehow I already know this isn't real. To be fair I was somehow aware of how unreal all the fabulous falsities in my early death dreams were but this was different. I am lying in bed, looking up at the ceiling. I have just came out of a deep sleep but everything around me still feels like a dream and the common sense of familiarity I had been feeling was completely gone.

I feel totally lost but somehow I know this is my home. I am sleeping in a king size bed but there is no one next to me, although the empty space on the bed still holds the warmth and shape of a body that had been occupying it recently. My eyes are fuzzy and the air in the room is wavy.

I stand up and walk over to the wash room, splash some cold water in my face and focus on my own image in the mirror. I look clearly older than any age my actual self made it to. I hear some mumbling and slight banging coming from the lower part of the house.

Walking through the house I know exactly where I am going although I feel like I have never been here before. Pictures on the walls throughout the hallway show a happy family. Myself, a beautiful woman and an adorable young daughter. Baby pictures, family portraits, vacation memories, birthdays....the hallways are a shrine to things that never were and never will be. Smiles so real on the faces of my family, my family that I destroyed before it even came to fruition.

Downstairs in the kitchen my wife is alive. My daughter is alive. My mother and father are in their 70's and they are alive. My mother is cutting up fruit at the kitchen table and my dad is reading the paper.

My wife hands me a cup of coffee and kisses me on the neck, the same way she did at crobar back in 1991. I can hear the opening chords of drown in my ears "no matter where you are, I can still hear you when you drown" The way she kissed me with the very tip of her lips, almost teasing me...it was one of the ways I used to be sure I was still alive no matter how terrible things in my life were going. Two lips and hot breathe. A tangible expression of love and lust and in this death dream I could actually feel the kiss.

I greet my mother with a kiss and pat my dad on the back. Good morning.

Amazing morning.

I walk out into the family room where my daughter is on the floor playfully teasing her little puppy, Mikey #2. This is my little girl. Such a beautiful living incarnation of the love her mother and I shared. A wonderful creation that never was. Her eyes burned with my passion and her smile held her mother's compassion and heart song.

If it would have been possible for my heart to break anymore, this would have been the moment.

My daughter looks up at me and I look right back at her both of us smiling. An unspoken love can sometimes be even more powerful than one constantly voiced. When you can feel a mutual love by just looking into another being's eyes, words become meaningless. Time stops. I wish it would stop forever, right here.

I step out onto the back porch and gaze at our backyard. Trees and field for as far as the eyes can see. We are certainly not in Chicago anymore. Maybe it's the suburbs...maybe it's Vermont, I could honestly care less. I turn back around, sipping my coffee, looking back into my house through the floor to ceiling glass windows.

I look at the calendar on the kitchen wall.

2002.

My daughter is still playing with Mikey #2 and he is furiously licking her face like its some kind of tasty treat and she is giggling in the most adorable way. I take a deep breathe and another sip of my coffee. I can taste the coffee, feel its heat on my lips, then down my throat and into my stomach. I can actually feel it moving through my body like its actually, really happening.

Watching my daughter play with our dog, like it is actually, really happening.

Thinking, wow, this would have been nice.

Sometimes people change. They don't want to but they do.

As usual, everything around me starts to fade to an almost nothingness and as this is happening I cry inside my dream for the first time. I cry because I don't know what is going to come next. I want to keep waking up and living this moment but I am afraid that I will just keep shifting between these memories and alternate realities and it will never end.

As my daughter, wife, mother and father disappear I am left in an empty house. Soon enough, the house is gone and I am once again in the familiar void between life and memory. In an instant all I see is a big black cloud of all my memories mixed together. It's like when you have a bunch of paint and mix it all together...it's not quite black, but a cloud or an essence of what black would be if it was really a color.

THE END

NOTES ON THIS PIECE:

THIS STORY WAS WRITTEN SHORTLY AFTER THE DEATH OF MY COUSIN ERIC MARK NELSON. HE DIED AT 30 YEARS OLD, ONE OF THE MOST ENERGETIC AND CREATIVE PEOPLE TO EVER BREATHE. HIS YOUNG PASSING INSPIRED ME TO THINK ON DEATH FOR A SHORT WHILE. I WROTE IN QUICK SPURTS AND THEN IGNORED IT FOR QUITE SOME TIME UNTIL THE WINTER OF 2012 WHEN I STARTED TO WRITE MY FIRST FULL LENGTH NOVEL. I REVISITED THIS SHORT STORY FOR INSPIRATION, MADE A FEW EDITS AND THEN LET IT SIT FOR A WHILE AGAIN. THE FINAL EDITS AND ADDITIONS WERE MADE ON MARCH 22ND OF 2013. I KNOW IT'S NOT PERFECT OR EVEN REALLY RELEVANT BUT SOMETHING ABOUT IT STILL CLICKS WITH ME 2 YEARS AFTER FIRST PUTTING THE WORDS DOWN ONE KEY AT A TIME.

LORRAINE'S DINER AT CHICAGO AND DAMEN, WHICH REALLY DID GIVE ME FOOD POISONING CLOSED IN JANUARY OF 2013. IT IS NOW A "MODERN" TACO JOINT CALLED METRO OR SOMETHING.

WHEN I FIRST STARTED TO WRITE THIS STORY I WAS LIVING ON THE NORTHWEST SIDE OF CHICAGO WITH A LESBIAN AND A CAT NAMED HANK DIRECTLY OFF OF THE KIMBALL BROWN LINE STOP OF THE CHICAGO TRANSIT AUTHORITY'S TRAIN SYSTEM. IN 1991 I WAS 4 YEARS OLD. NONE OF THE PEOPLE OR SITUATIONS IN THIS STORY ARE IN ANY WAY BASED ON REAL LIFE (BESIDES LORRAINE'S DINER GIVING ME FOOD POISONING WHICH I ONCE AGAIN WILL REMIND YOU, DID ACTUALLY HAPPEN). MY DAD NEVER KILLED MY DOG AND MY

PARENTS ARE STILL ALIVE AND HAPPILY MARRIED, LIVING IN WISCONSIN. I WOULD LIKE TO THANK THEM FOR THEIR CONSTANT LOVE AND SUPPORT BECAUSE I OBVIOUSLY WASN'T THE EASIEST CHILD TO RAISE.

ALSO, EVERYONE IS ENCOURAGED TO LISTEN TO THE ALBUM WHICH CONTAINS THIS PIECES NAMESAKE "SO YOUR BIG BLACK CLOUD WILL COME". THE ALBUM IS BY MOUNT EERIE AND IT IS CALLED "SINGERS". IT IS ONE OF THE MOST BEAUTIFUL COLLECTIONS OF SIMPLE HEARTFELT SONGS EVER RECORDED. PLEASE ENJOY IT.

"HOW DO YOU LIVE AND FORGET THAT YOU DIE" - MOUNT EERIE - "HUMAN"

"YOU'RE NOT DEAD, YOU'RE FREE" - MOUNT EERIE - "I CAN'T BELIEVE YOU ACTUALLY DIED"

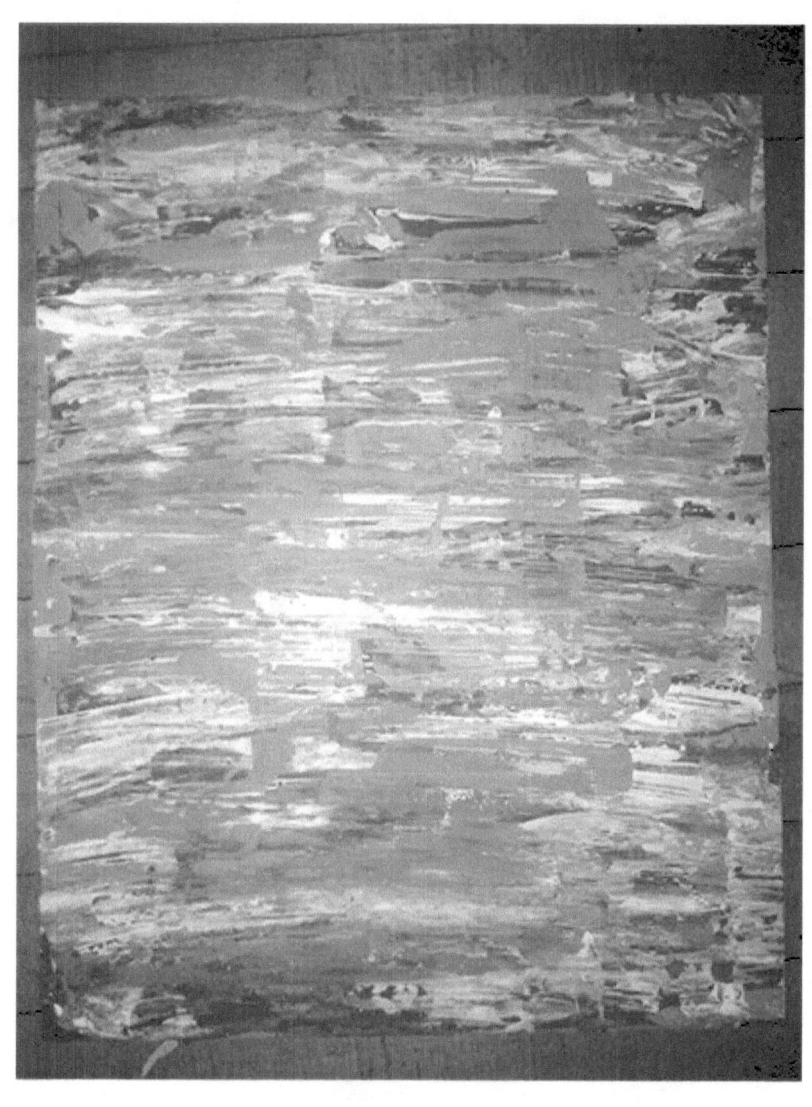

INTO

GAY

CRUISING

?

A SMALL COLLECTION OF STORIES ABOUT SUICIDE

SMALL FINGERS

I am trying to reinvent myself.

I was never totally pleased with how I was invented to began with. Lanky with pale skin, tiny hands with small fingers. Bad lungs. Even worse posture. A natural slouch in my stance and a constant stabbing pain in my back for as long as I can remember. I was born early and came out backwards with my feet first. My father always liked to make wise ass cracks about this. About how I was trying to fight to stay inside my mother.

About how I was born a mama's boy.

My father is dead now. I still live at home.

No job.

No motivation.

Poor health.

No friends.

No communication.

A broken self.

I like to read books and escape into the stories. I like to read a segment and then lay back and close my eyes and pretend I am living what the words are laying out. It feels good for a second but then I have to open my eyes and return to my actual life. A series of uninteresting events that constantly numbs me to the core.

A bowl of cereal.

A painful piss.

Twelve hours straight on the internet.

A self induced climax.

A short nap.

Fighting the urge to kill myself.

Back when I was in high school I met several kids with dreams and goals. I met people who wanted to be someone, wanted to go somewhere. People who wanted to get out of our small town. People who wanted to go to college and get real jobs. People who wanted to move to the big city and become superstars. People who wanted to make a difference in the world. I have never had any of these feelings or desires. I have never wanted to be or do anything. I simply am.

Never dreamed of a better life.

Never asked for anything.

Never went anywhere.

I am trying to reinvent myself before it's too late. If a person can be reinvented. I can't imagine growing old the way I am. I can't imagine growing old at all. What will happen to me when my mother passes away? I will have no home, I will be thrown into the streets. I should get a job. I should go back to school, make friends, get a haircut. I should start listening to music and watching TV so I have something to talk about with people. I should just go outside just to go outside.

Too little too late.

I have become what I am.

Done all I ever wanted to do.

Had no goals.

and I accomplished them.

I am trying to reinvent myself.

The only way to start completely new is to put an end to it.

You can't start a story over without erasing what you already wrote.

You can't draw a new picture on your etch-a-sketch without shaking the fucking thing first.

Maybe someday I will write another letter like this and it will be much different. In another life. With another, more capable body and a clear, less fragile mind. With a new name.

New York

I'm leaving for New York City tonight.

I have my bus ticket. Buses are much less regulated than planes. I have my ticket in my hand, in my hand which is trembling with a sweaty palm and tiny little hairs standing on edge all the way up my arm. I have packed only the essentials...2 pairs of slacks, one skirt, undergarments, 4 shirts, my toothbrush, a carton of cigarettes and my newly purchased copy of "Relocating to New York City and surrounding areas" by Ellen R. Shapiro. I am starting to think I am over thinking everything or maybe I didn't think enough to begin with.

I am delusional. I am seriously fucking sick and I need to seek help.

I sit down on the edge of my bed as I tuck the book into my duffel bag. I glance over at my boyfriend, Robert. He is laid out on the bed, naked as the day he was born, blood still fresh but now semi dry and no longer seeping from his neck. His eyes are still open but they are kind of rolled back up towards the top of his head like he is trying to stare at his own hair. Maybe I should feel something from all of this yet all I can think about is how bad I want a cigarette. I don't want to open the carton that is buried near the bottom of my duffel bag so I stretch my arm out over my dead boyfriend's body and reach for his nightstand and grab his half full pack. Marlboro red 100's. Fucking disgusting but it will have to do.

I light one up and take a long slow pull, holding in the smoke for as long as I possibly can before slowly exhaling with an audible noise of air coming from my mouth. A thought comes to my mind. One I can't believe just hit me now. I stand up and walk over to the other side of the room next to the side of the bed he is laying on. Grab his jeans and remove the wallet from his back pocket. 32 dollars.

"32 dollars is all you have in your fucking wallet?" I scream out loud to him like he can actually still hear me.

What a fucking loser. Fucking ill tempered, violent, misogynistic piece of shit. You got what you deserved. How many lives did you think you were going to ruin before it caught up with you. People like you think you are fucking invincible. Big tough guys who were always popular and never had to work for shit. Spent your youth getting laid and going to parties without a care in the world. Took every girlfriend you ever had for granted but never started beating or abusing them in any way until your early twenties. You piece of human shit.

I know that I won't last long. I already know that so I wish my fucking mind would stop screaming it at me. I am not going to New York to start a new life. I am going to New York because I have always wanted to see the greatest city in the world. I am going to New York to see the Empire state building and the statue of liberty and times square. I am going to New York to visit Central Park and Greenwich Village and that novelty restaurant in the west village where the staff is dressed in costumes from science fiction novels of the past. I am going to New York City because I want to and you would never take me.

I am going to New York City and when I have had my share of fun, I am going to fucking kill myself in the most spectacular way I can think of at the time.

TWENTY - ONE

Most of my life I thought I was happy. It was just the other day actually when I realized how severely fucked my life has been. I don't know exactly what happened to trip my mind into remembrance mode but all the sudden one night I was flooded with things from my past which I had subconsciously blocked. Things that make it really hard to keep living and force a smile.

When I was young my father touched me. Not just once, not just two or three times but on a regular basis for most of my early youth I was used as a sex toy for my drugged out, alcoholic, unemployed father. He had fibromyalgia and was on a constant dose of intense pain killers which he almost always mixed with tall cans of malt liquor. My mother left when I was three weeks old so I lived with my father and my aunt in a small 1 bedroom apartment.

My father and I shared the living room and my aunt stayed in the bedroom in the back of the apartment. When my aunt was younger she gave birth to a premature baby that died at about four and a half weeks old. This fucked her right up. She almost never leaves her room and constantly caries around a doll of a baby. I am sure there is a term for what's wrong with her but I have no fucking idea what to call it, so I just call her insane.

The sexual abuse from my father started at such a young age and was such a regular thing that I had no idea there was anything wrong with it.

When my father died, I was 10 years old. We were watching a movie on TV, I got up to go the bathroom and wash myself from his latest assault on me just moments earlier. I started hearing what sounded like gagging or choking coming from the living room so I ran back in. My fathers eyes were rolled into the back of his head and he was vomiting slowly...choking on clumps of it that couldn't make it past his throat. He was grasping his neck with one hand and bending forward on the couch reaching towards me for help with the other.

I just stood there.

I just felt like letting him die.

I continued to live with my aunt until the age of 16 when she discovered I was a lesbian and in a crazy fit of misplaced rage, she kicked me out into the streets. At this point all of the instances of abuse from my childhood had mostly been forgotten. My girlfriend and I ran away and hopped a bus to Baltimore to try and make it on the streets out there. We figured we had more of a chance in a big city, more people to beg from and more abandoned buildings and alleys to sleep in.

When I was 19 we had been living at a flophouse for about 6 months with a bunch of other users and abusers. One night when I was already asleep my girl decided to go to a party near union square to try and score some dope. She had a habit of fucking guys in exchange for drugs, I suppose I didn't mind since she always shared with me and ended up back next to me in our bed. This night turned out a bit different though. She ended up meeting a real charmer. This guy fucked her raw in an alley and then stuck a screwdriver through her head and left her body there next to a dumpster.

I am almost 21 now and I still live in a flophouse. This is the way I have been living most of my life. Sharing a living room in a one bedroom apartment with my sexually abusive father wasn't really that much different than sharing a 4 bedroom house with 16 drug addicts. Its just that for the first time ever I actually am feeling how sad I am and how sad I always have been. Death has taken everyone I ever loved from me.

Now I am giving myself to death. I want to see my girl again and as fucked up as it sounds, I want to see my junkie perverted father again too.

I'm sure hell is pretty similar to a flophouse and I know for certain that those I love will be waiting for me there.

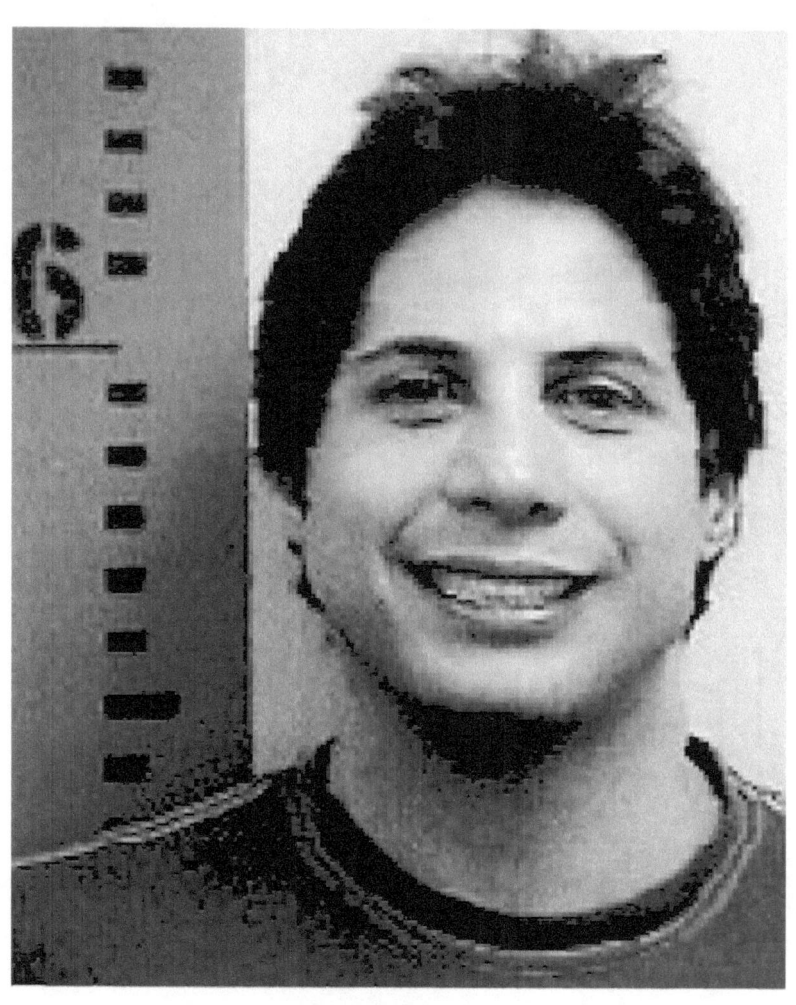

FEMINIST

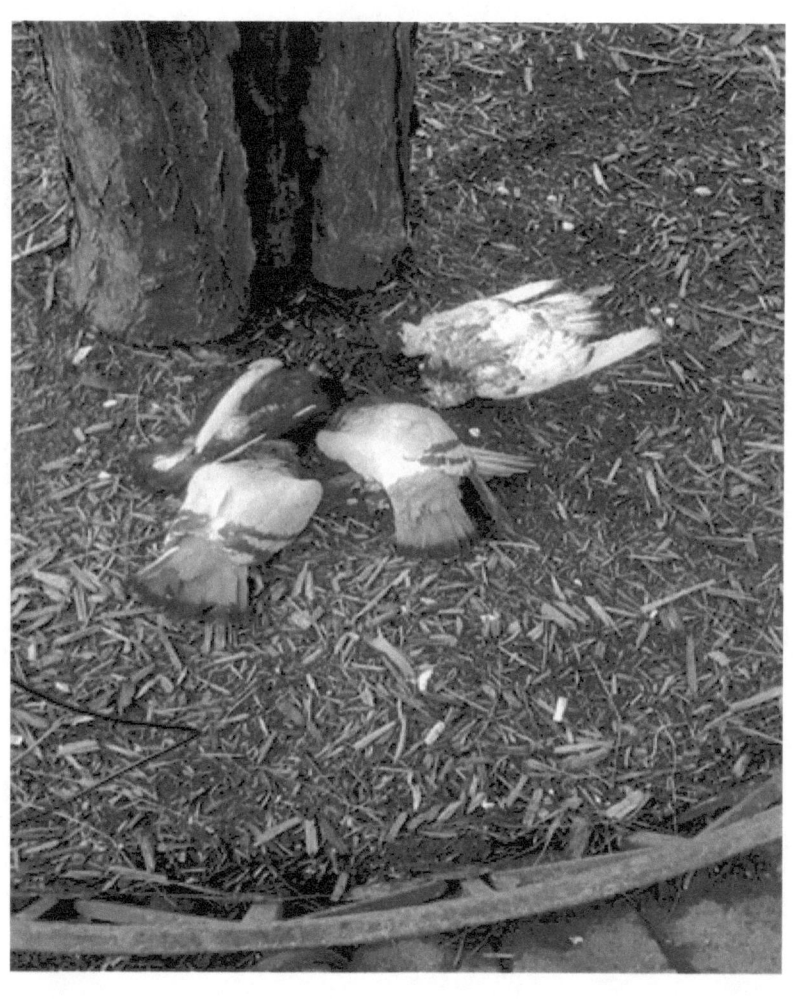

THE SHORTEST STORIES EVER TOLD

HAM AND CHEESE.

I was on the porch of the house I shared with my grandfather and I was shoving a ham and cheese sandwich down my throat. About halfway through the sandwich I began to choke on a rather large slice of the ham that had become lodged in my throat. I couldn't even muster enough oxygen to let out a small scream for help, so I fell to the wooden floor of the deck and began bashing and banging my hands and feet as hard as possible onto the ground until my alcoholic, diabetic, one armed grandfather came running out and immediately punched me in the stomach 3 times....when that didn't help, he reached his prosthetic arms fake hand right deep down into my throat and pulled out the chunk of ham like he was scooping ice cream at a soda shop.

I lived with my grandfather for as long as I could remember. My father was a schizophrenic who was convinced that he was some kind of powerful all knowing genius and that my mother was sent from outer space as some kind of spy for an alien race who was trying to absorb all of his knowledge, or some kind of absurd bullshit of that nature. Anyway, he supposedly killed my mother and then killed himself when I was around 3 months old. It took about 6 days for the cops to finally come and do a "well being" check at our house, which is when they found me half starved to death in the crib in my bedroom and both of my parents dead and decaying on the kitchen floor about 100 feet away.

The only family I had at all was my poor sad ass bastard grandfather who took me in with little hesitation, probably looking forward to having a small human that he could boss around and treat like shit with little to no consequence. I never met my grandmother and from what I understand no one else in the family ever got the chance to get to know her either. She died when my mother was about the same age I was when my mother herself died. It is suspected that my grandfather probably either beat her to death or poisoned her, all I ever remember him saying about her was that she never know when to keep her God damn mouth shut.

CUNNILINGUS.

PISSING
SHITTING
CUMMING
SWEATING
SNEEZING
BLEEDING
PUKING
CRYING

LIST OF THINGS I'VE DONE WRONG IN MY LIFE

-
-
-
-

ARE
YOU
FUCKED
?

One time I saw some guy passed out on the sidewalk in front of the rite aid by sunset and highland. He had pissed himself and the urine literally soaked through his pants and was running down the sidewalk. Less than 20 feet away they were filming an episode of some Nickelodeon show and some fat wasp lady with a clipboard was yelling about kosher deli trays. That's when I decided I wanted to spend the rest of my life in Los Angeles.

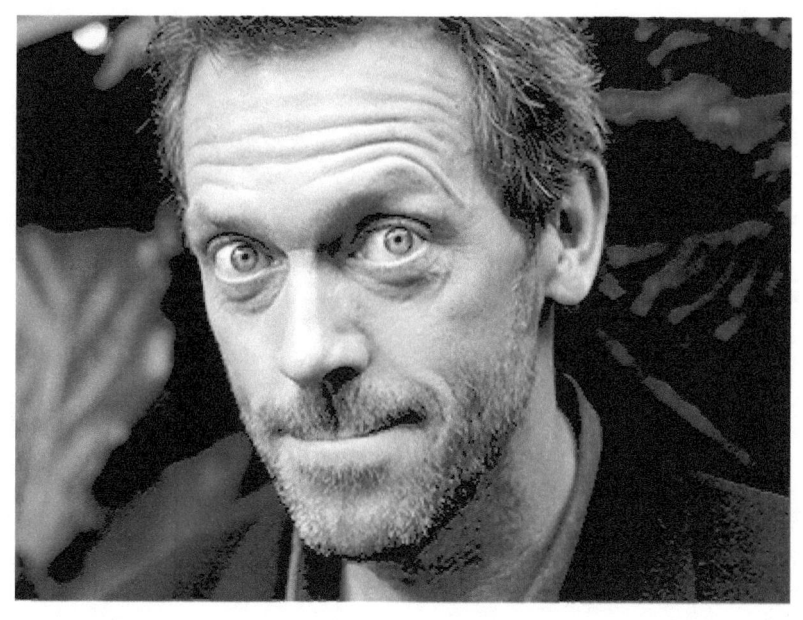

Television
Superstar
Huge Laurie

Lonely liver lovers live longer

I had a cousin who had really severe asthma. He was also sickly underweight and loved to masturbate. His poor health and obsession with self satisfaction landed him in the hospital over 100 times between the ages of 12 and 20. Every time he would jerk off he would work himself up so much that he would have an asthma attack. When he died at the age of 21 his mother found him naked, spread eagle and rigor mortis with his cock in his hand and a note near him on the floor that read "PLEASURE > PAIN".

At the funeral everyone cried and the Rabbi said some really nice things about him, leaving out the fact that he died holding his dick.

2 months later that Rabbi also died with his dick in his hand. He was found hanging from a belt with black on black lesbian porn playing on his computer.

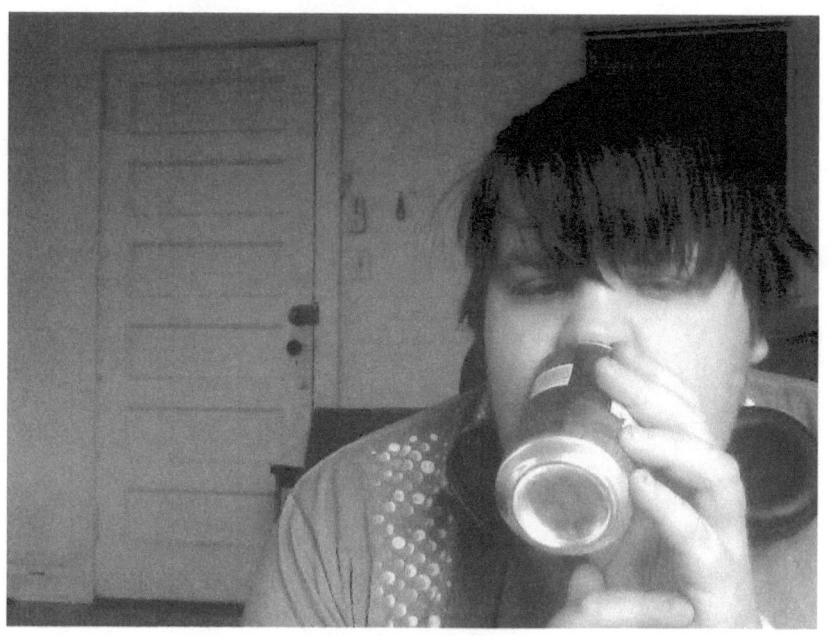

Jay Miller is a two-spirit living organism who makes art and has trouble sleeping. "Everything is fucked forever" is the first official release of his writings and art. Jay enjoys reading, drinking excessively and feminist pornography. He splits his time between Chicago, Los Angeles and Mid Michigan.

www.ingramcontent.com/pod-product-compliance
Lightning Source LLC
Chambersburg PA
CBHW020929180526
45163CB00007B/2942